Bernhard Pick

Historical Sketch of the Jews

Since the destruction of Jerusalem

Bernhard Pick

Historical Sketch of the Jews
Since the destruction of Jerusalem

ISBN/EAN: 9783744795791

Printed in Europe, USA, Canada, Australia, Japan

Cover: Foto ©Lupo / pixelio.de

More available books at **www.hansebooks.com**

HISTORICAL SKETCH

OF

THE JEWS,

SINCE THE DESTRUCTION OF
JERUSALEM.

BY
REV. BERNHARD PICK, Ph.D.

———

NEW YORK:
JOHN B. ALDEN, PUBLISHER.
1887.

HISTORICAL SKETCH

OF

THE JEWS.

Judæa was a waste, Jerusalem was a heap of
ruins. The temple had been consumed by
flames, and the third exile—the European—
began. Directly after the triumph of Titus,
the great Council of the Israelitish Rabbins was
established at Tiberias, in Galilee. The school
of Scribes, instituted in that city, soon took the
place of that temple, whose restoration has
never ceased to be the object of their hopes and
prayers. The celebrated revolt of Bar-Cochba
and Akiba sprung, in great measure, from
thence. Tiberias had become a kind of Jerusalem, where the so-called Oral Law was framed.
The first idea of such an undertaking is
thought by many to have originated with Rabbi
Akiba, who was flayed alive in the Bar-
Cochba revolt, in 135. But universal tradition
attributes both the plan and its accomplish-
ment to Rabbi Judah, the Holy, styled also the
Nasi, or Prince, that is to say, spiritual head

of the synagogues in that country. About the
year A. D. 190 he completed a collection of all
the oral or traditional laws, called the *Mishna*.
The later Rabbins have exhausted their in-
genuity in making commentaries upon, and
additions to, this work. The whole collection
of these commentaries is named *Gemara*.
With the *Mishna*, its text-book, it forms the
Talmuds. Of these the Jerusalem Talmud is
prior in date, having been completed toward
the end of the third century in Palestine;
while the Babylonian Talmud, compiled in
the schools of Babylon and Persia, takes its
date from the year 500. The Talmud is not
the only national work of which the Jews, during their present captivity, can boast. From
the very first we find ranked with it two other
works of tradition—the *Massorah* or fixing the
text of the Bible, and *Cabbala* or "Theosophy."
   The dispersed Jews, even before the fall of
erusalem, had classed themselves under three
different designations. The Rabbins under-
stand by the "Captivity of the East," the re-
mains of the ten tribes; by that "of Egypt,"
the Jews under the dominion of the Ptole-
mies, particularly those of Alexandria; by that
"of the West" the Jews dispersed over every
part of the Roman Empire. In the following

sketch we shall speak only of the Jews in the East, and in the West, in Asia and in Europe, since with the history of the Jews in those countries are connected the annals of their wandering and suffering in all parts of the world.

In the Roman Empire, after the reign of Vespasian and Adrian, the condition of the Jews was not only tolerable, but in many respects prosperous. But a complete reverse took place when the Emperor of Rome knelt before the Cross, and the Empire became a Christian state. From this epoch we may date the first period of humiliation. The second marked period in their state of moral and political degradation extends from the commencement of the middle ages to the death of Charlemagne and the incursions of the Normans in Europe. This period, which closes with the discovery of America, the reign of Charles V., and the Reformation, was for the Jews everywhere, with the exception of those in Spain and Portugal, a time of the deepest misery, oppression, and decay. Thus the period of cruel oppression of the Jews in the West began with the triumph of Christianity over Paganism, just as in the East, three centuries later, it may be dated from the rise and triumph of the Crescent. As has already been stated, the humiliation of the Jews commenced under Constantine. A gleam of hope shone upon them in the days of Julian the Apostate, but they were more ill-treated under his Christian successors. Till the reign of Theodosius, in the fourth century, however, their position in the Empire was tolerable. Different, however, it was in the fifth century. The Roman Empire had, from the year 395, been divided into the Eastern or Greek Empire, of which Constantinople was the capital; and the Western Empire, of which Rome and Italy still formed the center. In both these divisions, the position and treatment of the Jews became worse and worse. In the West, even under Honorius, its first emperor, oppressive laws began to be enacted against the Jews. In the East, *i. e.*, in the eastern part of the Roman Empire, soon after called the Empire of Greece, or Byzantium, the position of the Jews became particularly unfavorable. The government of the Emperor Justin, and the code of Justinian, soon permanently fixed the social relations of the Jews in the Byzantine Empire. Justin (A. D. 523) excluded all non-Christians from holding any office or dignity in the state. In the reign of Justinian the enactments against the Jews were made more onerous. No wonder that during his reign many rebellions broke out among the Jews.

From the reign of Justinian, the position of the Jews in the Greek Empire became such as to prevent their possessing any degree of political importance. True, they carried on theological studies in the country of their fathers, especially at Tiberias. But even here the last surviving gleam of their ancient glory was soon extinguished. The dignity of Patriarch had ceased to exist with the year 429, and the link connecting the different synagogues of the Eastern Empire was broken. Many Jews quitted Palestine and the Byzantine empire to seek refuge in Persia and Babylonia, where they were more favored. When in 1455 Constantinople was taken by the Turks, some of the Jewish exiles from Spain and Portugal took refuge in the ancient capital of the Eastern Empire, where the number of their descendants is now considerable.

In the far East, beyond the boundaries of the Grecian Empire, the Jews continued in a comparatively prosperous condition until the triumph of the Islam was complete. The Jews in Babylonia were governed by the *Resh-Glutha*, or Prince of the Captivity. Since the Babylonian exile a great many Jews had settled

here, who were joined by several fresh colonies even before the destruction of Jerusalem
by Titus, and by many more after that epoch.
The Prince of the Captivity mediated between
the heads of the synagogue and the Persian or
Parthian kings. The dignity itself took its
rise while the Parthians reigned in Persia, and
continued under the new dynasty of the Sas-
sanides, and only came to an end in the
middle of the eleventh century, under the
dominion of the caliphs. The feeling existing
between the Parthian kings and the Jews was
of a very friendly nature, and whenever the
Parthians undertook a war against the Romans, the common foe of both Jews and
Parthians, the former always assisted the latter. Thus when Chosroes I., surnamed the
Great, declared war against the Byzantine
Empire in 531, the Jews lent their assistance.
And although their hopes were for the present
crushed by the brilliant victory gained by the
Romans, yet under Chosroes II., grandson of
the former, 25,000 Jews assisted in the war
against Heraclius, which resulted in the capture
of Jerusalem (A. D. 625), which was, however,
retaken by Heraclius four years later. Under
the caliphs, the Jews met by turns with good
and ill treatment. The downfall of the caliphs

brought no favorable change to the Jews. On
the contrary, their troubles increased and their
celebrated schools at Pumbaditha and Sora
at length entirely disappeared, and the succes-
sion of their learned men was continued hence-
forth in Spain. Thus the rise of the Mohammedan power in Asia gave the signal that the
time for their greatest oppression and degradation in the East also had come.

In the Peninsula of Arabia the Jews had
dwelt from time immemorial. They date
their establishment there, according to some,
from the visit of the Queen of Sheba to Solomon. Before the time of Mohammed the
Jews were very prosperous there, and even a
Jewish kingdom under Jewish kings should
have had existed there. When Mohammed
made his appearance, he found the Jews in
general favorably disposed toward him.
Several of the Jewish tribes became even his
open partisans. But when his principles and
plans became more thoroughly known, and the
Jews rejected him, Mohammed at once commenced a war of extermination against them.
His first attack was against the clan of the
Beni-Kinouka, who dwelt in Medina, and was
overcome by the warrior-prophet. The same
fate awaited the other tribes, one after the

other. From the moment that the Jews declared themselves against Mohammed, they
became the especial object of his hatred, and
since that time a feeling of enmity has ever
existed between the Mussulman and the Jew.
Crescent and Cross shared equally in the contempt and hatred of the Jew, and as in
Christian Europe so in Mohammedan Asia and
Africa, the Jew was compelled to bear a dis-
tinctive mark in his garments—*here* the yellow
hat, *there* the black turban.

Beyond the boundaries of either the old
Roman or the Byzantine Empire, Jews have,
in early times, been met with, both in the
most remote parts of the interior of Asia, and
upon the coast of Malabar. In the latter place
they probably arrived in the fifth century in
consequence of a persecution raised in Persia.
In the seventeenth century a Jewish colony
was met with in China. When the Jews
emigrated there is difficult to ascertain.

But to return to the West. It has already
been stated that with the conversion of the
Roman Empire to Christianity evil days came
upon the Jews. In the Western Empire this
unfavorable change commenced in the days
of Honorius, and would have continued so;
but the storm that burst over Rome toward

the end of the fifth century changed in a degree the position of the Jews. The Northern nations, as long as they professed Arianism in preference to the Catholic faith, showed themselves merciful to their Jewish subjects. This was especially the case with the Goths. When the dominion of the Ostrogoths, under their king Theodoric, succeeded that of Odoacer and the Heruli in Italy and the West, the Jews had every reason to be satisfied with their new sovereign. The consequence was that the Goths in the West, like the Persians in the East, found faithful allies in the Jews of that period. When Justinian, by his general, Narses, conquered Italy from the Ostrogoths (A.D. 555), the Jews, especially those at Naples, assisted him, only to be heavily punished afterward.

The Visigoths also, in their defence of Arles in Provence, against the Franks under Clovis, were assisted by the Jews. In Spain, the kings of the Visigoths treated them with favor, till about the year C00, their king Recared, having embraced Catholicism, inaugurated that peculiar system of conduct toward the Jews, which finally resulted in their total expulsion from the Peninsula. The Franks were at the beginning less merciful

to the Jews than the Goths. The Merovin-
gians treated them with peculiar rigor. Thus
in 540, King Childebert forbade the Jews to
appear in the streets of Paris, during the
Easter week. Clotaire II. deprived them of
the power of holding office. King Dagobert
compelled them either to receive baptism or
to leave the country. Under the Carlovingians
in France, the Jews of the eighth and ninth
centuries enjoyed a great degree of prosperity,
so that the Romish bishops took alarm.
Under Pepin *le Bref*, they enjoyed many
privileges, and so likewise under his son Charlemagne, and under his successor and son
Louis *le Débonnaire*. The latter even freed
them, from the grinding taxes imposed upon
them, and confirmed to them these immunities
in the year 830. And all exertions of the
priesthood, especially of Agobard, bishop of
Lyons, to injure the Jews, were utterly useless.

The position of the Jews underwent an entire change at the downfall of the Carlovingian
dynasty, which began to decay after the death
of Louis *le Débonnaire*. The invasion of the
Normans was partly the cause, and partly the
signal for a complete change of kings in
Europe. An age of barbarism spread over the
whole face of Christianity, the feudal system

developed itself, in every way injurious to the
Jews. But one of the greatest evils which
they were compelled to endure, was the prev-
alence of the crusading spirit. During the
first crusade (1096-1099), Treves, Spires,
Worms, Mayence, Cologne, and Regensburg
were the seat of oppression, murders, and bod-
ily tortures, inflicted upon the Jews. During
the second crusade (1147–1149), Rudolph, a
fanatical monk, traveling through central Europe, stirred up the populace to take vengeance
on all unbelievers. The cry "Hep! hep!" was
sufficient to bring terror to the heart of every
Jew. But King Conrad III. and such men as
Bernard of Clairvaux protected them, and
thus the sufferings of the Jews were less,
compared with the intemperate zeal of Rudolph. During the middle ages, the Jews
were not only persecuted, but, where they
were tolerated, they became also the Pariahs
of the West. But to resume the thread of
events.

In France, formerly so signally patronized
by the Carlovingians, the Jews experienced a
different treatment after the extinction of that
dynasty. Toward the end of the eleventh
century they were banished and afterward
recalled by Philip I. In 1182 they were at

first banished by Philip Augustus, but re-
admitted upon certain conditions, one of
which was the obligation to wear a little wheel
upon their dress as a mark. Louis VII.
(A. D. 1223) treated them all as his serfs, and
with one stroke of his pen remitted to his
Christian subjects all their debts to the Jews.
Louis IX. (St. Louis), being anxious to con-
vert them, commanded that the Talmud be
destroyed by fire, and twenty-four carts-full
of the Talmud were publicly burned in Paris
(1244). Philip the Fair, after robbing them
repeatedly, expelled the Jews from France in
1306. Under Louis X. they were treated un-
favorably, while Philip V., the Long, favored
and protected them. In 1341 the usual accusations of treason, poisoning the wells, etc., were
brought against them, and many were burned,
massacred, banished, or condemned to heavy
fines. Under John II. they enjoyed a little
rest, and so also under Charles V. But in
1370 they were again banished, but soon recalled under Charles VI. In spite of the many
vicissitudes, Jewish learning flourished in
France, especially in the south. Men like
David Kimchi and Rashi have become house-
hold names in Jewish as well as in Christian
theology.

In England the Jews date their first residence from the time of the Heptarchy. In the twelfth century, under Henry II. and his son, the cruel treatment and plundering of the Jews reached its height. On the coronation day of King Richard I. (1189), when they came to pay their homage, the population plundered and murdered them a whole day and night in London. This sad example of London was followed at Stamford, Norwich, and more especially at York. Under King John (A. D. 1199) all kinds of liberties and privileges were granted to the Jews, but he soon showed that he cared more for their money than for their persons. Henry III. (1217–1272) followed the same policy, and when the Jews petitioned the king to allow them to leave the country, he would not grant that request. Under Edward I. they were banished in 1290, and some sixteen thousand are said to have left the country.

In Germany, Jews were found already in the fourth century, especially at Cologne, where they soon became numerous and prosperous. But the commencement of the middle ages in Germany, as elsewhere, put an end to their favorable position. It is true that the Emperor of Germany regarded the Jews as his

Kammerknechte, or "Servants of the Imperial Chamber," and as such they enjoyed the emperor's protection, but the scores of violent deeds, which are recorded, only show that even the protection of the emperor could not prevent the popular rage from breaking out and marking its course by bloodshed and desolation. The least cause was sufficient to massacre the Jews. When in 1348 an epidemic malady, known as the *Black Death,* visited half of Europe, the Jews were blamed for it because they were said to have poisoned the wells and rivers. A general massacre took place, in spite of the demonstrations of princes, magistrates, bishops, and the Pope himself. In the south of Germany and in Switzerland, the persecution raged with most violence. From Switzerland to Silesia, the land was drenched with innocent blood, and in some places their residence was forbidden.

In the Netherlands, the history of the Jews during the middle ages was much like that of Germany and the north of France. In Flanders they were already living at the time of the Crusaders. In the twelfth century they were driven out, but were found there again in the fourteenth. In 1370 they were accused of having pierced the holy wafer, an accusation which had brought many to the stake. In Utrecht the Jews resided till the year 1444. In Holland, Zealand, and Fries-land, many Jews had sought refuge after their banishment from France by Philip the Fair.

Before the end of the tenth century, Jews are already found at Prague. Boleslaus I. favored them, and permitted them to build a synagogue. In Poland they existed very early. Under Boleslaus V., Duke of Po-land (1264), they enjoyed many privileges. His great-grandson, King Casimer, showed them still greater favor, out of love, it is said, for Esther, a beautiful Jewess. Synagogues, academies, and rabbinical schools have always abounded in Poland.

In Italy, where Jews have resided from early times in their *ghettos*, the Popes generally appeared kindly toward them. Gregory I., the Great, in the seventh century, proved himself the friend of the Jews, but Gregory VII., in the tenth century, was their enemy. In other great towns of Italy, the position of the Jews varied. At Leghorn and Venice they met with favor, and so also with a less degree in Florence, but at Genoa they were looked upon with enmity. In the kingdom of Naples,

where they settled about the year 1200, persecutions took place from time to time. Italy is
the home of some Jewish poets and expositors.

In Spain the Jews must have settled at a
very early time, for the Council of Elvira,
assembled in 305, made enactments against
them, which proves that they had already
become numerous there. Under Recared, the
first Catholic sovereign of the Gothic race, the
long-continued and relentless work of persecution began. His successor Sisebul (612–617)
ordered all his Jewish subjects to renounce
their faith or quit his dominions. Under
Sisenard, the fourth Council of Toledo, in
the year 631, mitigated these measures of com-
pulsion, without rescinding any of the penal-
ties which had been previously enacted.
Chintilla, in 626, exiled the Jews, but they
still remained in great numbers under Wamba
(672). In 698, Erwig persecuted them, while
Egiza banished them upon the accusation of
having entered into league with the Saracens
of Africa. Witzia (in 700) recalled them.
Under his successor Rodrigo, the Saracens
invaded Spain after the famous battle of
Xeres de la Frontera in 711. The Jews
greeted the Arabs as their deliverers, who
again treated them kindly. In the reign of

Abderahman III. (912–961), Cordova became eminent for industry and learning, and the Jews shared largely in the splendor and prosperity of the Arabs. Less peaceful times, however, enjoyed the Jews in the Christian states of the Peninsula.

From the southern part of Spain the Jews had emigrated to Castile in the eleventh and twelfth centuries, where they soon became very prosperous. Their synagogues and schools increased, and as formerly in the East by the *Resh Glutha*, so were they now governed by the Rabbin mayor, an Israelite, usually in favor at court, and appointed by the king. Every kind of office was open to them, and they often served in the army. But soon the populace, stirred up by the inferior clergy, gave vent to envy, which manifested itself first by the usual accusations of sacrilege and the murder of Christian children, but soon broke out into open rage and acts of violence. Amid the general prosperity of the Jewish nation, a massacre took place at Toledo in 1212, and in 1213 the Council of Zamora, in Leon, vehemently demanded the revival and enforcement of the ancient law against the Jews. In general we may say, that the kings of Castile and Aragon, with

very few exceptions, eminently befriended
the Jews during the four centuries which
elapsed between the reign of Ferdinard I. and
the Catholic sovereigns, Ferdinand and Isabella. Ferdinand I. was almost the only one
who showed enmity to the Jews. Alphonso
VI. (who conquered Toledo from the Saracens) granted many valuable privileges to the
Jews. Alphonso IX., of Castile (A. D. 1158–
1196), showed them still greater favor, because
of his love for the fair Jewess Rachel. The
prosperity of the Jews in Castile and their
influence reached its greatest height in the
reigus of Alphonso XI. (1312–1350) and his
son, Peter the Cruel (1350–1369). All this
grandeur and these privileges were, nevertheless, not unfrequently accompanied by violent acts on the part of the populace, and
complaints and protestations from the Councils
and the Cortes, which had little or no effect
upon the kings.

More perilous times, however, commenced
for the Jews of Castile and the rest of Spain
under John I. (1379–80). This king found
occasion to deprive them of the jurisdiction
they had hitherto possessed. Under Hnrey
III., tumults took place at Seville in 1390 and
1391 and the Jewish quarter was attacked and

burned to ashes. This fearful example spread, as by contagion, to Cordova, Madrid, Toledo, over the whole of Catalonia, and even to the isle of Majorca. In the first years of the reign of John II., a royal mandate, dated Valladolid, 1412, was issued, which contained the most oppressive measures which had ever been promulgated against the Jews since the time of the later Visigothic kings. Among other enactments, they were ordered to wear a peculiar dress. In consequence of these severe enactments, many joined the Church, who were styled *Conversos*, or "New Christians."

The glorious period during which Isabella, the sister of Henry IV., with her husband, Don Ferdinand of Aragon, governed Castile, brought a complete change over the whole face of the country, and became to the Jews, and also to the New Christians, the time of a most striking crisis.

But before speaking of this period, let us glance at some of the most famous literary men of the Jews during their residence in that country, before the close of the middle ages. We mention Menahem ben Saruk (d. 970), author of a biblical dictionary; Jehudah Ibn Chajug (in Arabic Aboulwalid), the chief of Hebrew grammarians (about 1050); Ibn

Ganach (d. 1050), the grammarian; Ibn Gabirol (the Avicebron among the Schoolmen), philosopher, grammarian, and commentator (d.1070); Ibn Pakuda the moralist (1050–1100) ; Ibn Giath, the cosmographer, astronomer, and philosopher; Ibn Gikatilla the grammarian (1070–1100;) Ibn Balaam, commentator and philologist (d. 1100); Moses ibn Ezra, the hymnist (d. 1139); Jehuda Ha-Levi, the philosopher and poet (d. 1141); Ibn Daud, the historian (d. 1180); Abraham ibn Ezra, commentator, philosopher, and poet (d. 1167); Jehuda Alcharizi, the Horace of Jewish poetry in Spain (d. 1230); Benjamin Tudela, the traveler; Jehuda Tibbon, the prince of translators (d. 1190); Isaac Alfasi (d.1089); Moses Maimonides, the greatest of all mediæval rabbis (d. 1204); Moses Gerundensis, or Nachmanides (d. 1270); Abraham Abulafia, the cabbalist (d. 1292); Moses ben Shem—Tob de Leon—the author of the *Sohar* (d. 1305); Jedaja Bedarchi, or Penini (d. 1340); Abner, of Burgos, better known by his Christian name *Alfonso Burgensis de Valladolid* (d. 1346); Jacob ben Asheri; Ibn Caspi (d. 1340); Gersonides, or Ralbaj among the Jews, famous as philosopher and commentator (d.1345). Solomon Levi of Burgos better known by his Christian name Paulus Burgensis or de

Santa Maria, bishop of Burges (d. 1435); Josef Albo (d.1444); Simon Duran, the polemic (d. 1444); Ibn Verga, the historian, who died in the dungeon of the Inquisition; Abravanel, the theologian and commentator, who was exiled with his co-religionists from Spain (d. 1515).

The great prosperity of the Jews in Spain proved their ruin. The ignorant populace, instigated by the priests, could not brook the happy condition of the Jews, and wherever they were to be found, they were from time to time pounced upon; numbers of them were slain, while others, to save their lives, submitted to baptism. Thus the Spanish Church contained, besides a body of real Jewish converts, whose names are known by their excellent writings, a large number of nominal Christians who, by sentiment, remained Jews. Soon popular suspicion was aroused against these latter, the so-called " New Christians;" and at last the Inquisition was set in motion to find those out who while outwardly conforming to the Church, secretly lived according to the rules of the Synagogue. Horrible are the details of what the Inquisition wrought at that time in Spain; but, curiously enough, all to no purpose. Cruel as was the old Inquisition, it was to be surpassed by the new Inquisition, established by Ferdinand and Isabella, and which cast so dark a shadow over their reign. While the old Inquisition was of a limited power, and its influence of little importance, the powers of the "New Inquisition" or "Holy Tribunal" were enlarged and extended, and under Torquemada, the first Inquisitor-General, it became one of the most formidable engines of destruction which ever existed. Isabella at first felt great repugnance to the establishment of this institution, and some of the most eminent men opposed it. But the Dominicans had set their heart upon it, and were determined to obtain it. What finally determined the queen to adopt it was a vow she had made when a young infanta, in the presence of Thomas of Torquemada, then her confessor, that if ever she came to the throne she would maintain the Catholic faith with all her power, and extirpate heresy to the very root; and thus it was that she became instrumental in the perpetration of the most horrible cruelties which blacken and deform the history of men. The New Inquisition reached its climax in the year 1492, when an edict was published ordering all Jews who would not embrace Christi-

anity to leave the country within four months.
The news of this edict came upon the Jews
like a thunder-clap. Every appeal to the
compassion of the king and queen was de-
feated by the opposition of Torquemada
The Jews offered immense sums of money as
a price for remaining in a country where they
had already been established for centuries.
But the merciless Torquemada presented himself before the king, with a crucifix in his
hand, and asked, for how many pieces of silver
more than Judas he would sell his Saviour to
the Jews? Over 300,000 Jews left Spain, and
emigrated to Africa, Italy, and Turkey. Most
of them went to Portugal, where they enjoyed a few years of rest. In 1497, however,
they were again left to the choice, either to
receive baptism or leave the country forever.
Many abandoned forever the soil of Portugal;
others, not few in number, embraced or feigned
to embrace the Roman Catholic faith   Under
Don Emanuel and his son John III., the
"New Christians" enjoyed the protection of
the state in every way in Portugal.

Following the Spanish exiles, a short time
after the edicts of 1492 and 1497, Jews and
New Christians were to be met with in the
newly-discovered territories of America and

in Brazil. In Africa, Asia, and the Turkish
Empire, their families and synagogues have
been established, and have continued to this
day. In great numbers the exiled Jews set
tled in the western parts of Africa, especially
in the states of Morocco. At Tripoli, Tunis,
Algiers, Oran, and Fez, Jews soon felt themselves at home. In the Turkish Empire,
soon after the taking of Constantinople by
the Turks, in 1453, the Jews became a promi-
nent part of the population, and when the
Spanish exiles came here, they found numer
ous synagogues and schools of learning. And
although they belonged to one nation, yet
they kept distinct from their co-religionists,
preserving not only their own liturgy, but
also their language, and were distinguished
here as everywhere from their other co-relig
ionists by the name of *Sephardin* or Span-
iards. In Italy also they were welcomed,
with the exception of Naples, where they were
not allowed to remain. In the Ecclesiastical
States, and especially at Rome, the exiles were
but little persecuted, and the New Christians
lived in far greater security in the Papal States
than in Spain and Portugal. The Jews established in Italy printing establishments; the
most celebrated was that at Ferrara, where

the famous Spanish version of the Old Testament was printed. That there were also many learned men among the Jews of Italy is but natural.

Shortly after the passing of the edicts in 1492 and 1497, many Jewish emigrants sought refuge on the northern side of the Pyrenees, where they enjoyed many privileges. Early in the seventeenth century, Portuguese Jews were settled and flourishing in the Danish States. At Hamburg, which was soon honored with the appellation of "Little Jerusalem," the Jews enjoyed a very great social prosperity. The country, however, which has shown the greatest favor and afforded the warmest hospitality to the exiled Spanish Jews since the close of the sixteenth century, was the Low Countries of the Netherlands. When the first Jews, or New Christians, from Spain, made their appearance in the Low Countries, there was not a vestige of those French and German Jews whose troubles we have before related. The first indication of this reëstablishment of the Jews in the southern part of the United Provinces is found in the year 1516. At that time some refugees from Spain petitioned Charles V. to be allowed to reside in his dominions. Their appeal

was unheeded, and severe edicts entirely excluded New Christians from Holland. And
yet, notwithstanding these edicts, many Jews
were to be found in these provinces before
and after their separation from Spain. Their
religion had long ceased to be tolerated, but
they practiced it with the greatest secrecy,
and lived and prospered under Spanish names.
At Antwerp, also, the concealed Jews were
very numerous, and had established academies for the study of Hebrew and Spanish
literature. Most of these Spanish and Portuguese Jewish families established themselves
shortly afterward in the Protestant Low
Countries, to seek there complete freedom for
the exercise of their own religion. Their first
settlement at Amsterdam was made on the
side of East Friesland. It was from Emb-
den, that, in the year 1594, ten individuals
of the Portuguese families of Lopes, Homen,
and Pereira came to Amsterdam, where they
soon resumed their original Jewish name of
Abendana, and in the year 1596 the Great
Day of Atonement was celebrated by a small
community of Portuguese Jews at Amsterdam. In 1598 they built the first synagogue
in that capital, and in 1618 the third. In the
meantime the German and Polish Jews had

also established their synagogues in the capital of Holland; and Amsterdam, like Hamburg,
was a "Little Jerusalem." Of the authors
and learned men brought up in the synagogues
of Holland, we mention Rabbi Menasseh Ben
Israel, who pleaded the cause of his brethren
before Oliver Cromwell. Contemporary with
him was the well known Uriel da Costa. To
the generation which succeeded that of Uriel
da Costa, belongs Benedict Spinoza. At the
Hague too, the Portuguese Jews enjoyed great
prosperity and esteem, and their synagogue
is situated in one of the finest quarters of the
town.

Almost immediately after the discovery of
the New World, the Jews from the Peninsula
established themselves in America. The first
Jewish colony was established in Brazil, in
1624, when the Dutch took possession of that
country. The nucleus formed by the Jewish
settlers from Holland was greatly strengthened
by the progress of the Dutch in Brazil, under
William of Nassau, about 1640, when some
600 Jews sailed from Amsterdam to Brazil in
1641, but who were obliged to leave again in
consequence of the downfall of the Dutch rule
in Brazil, in 1654. In the meantime, the
settlement founded in French Guiana in-

creased at a rapid rate, where the Jews enjoyed special privileges. During the wars
between France and England in the reign of
Louis XIV., the Jews in Eastern Guiana
suffered severely, in consequence of which
they settled at Surinam. Their privileges
were confirmed under King Charles II., by
Lord Willoughby (1662), and the Dutch and
West Indian Company. Of those parts of the
West Indies where Jewish settlements are
to be found, the British colony of Jamaica
deserves special mention. Here a large Hebrew congregation has been in existence since
the middle of the seventeenth century.

As regards the Jews in the United States and
North America at large, Prof. Cassel (in his
article *Juden* in Ersch and Gruber's *Allgemeine
Encyklopädie*) disposes of those of North
America in the following pithy words :—

"To the Jews emigrated to America, especially to the
United states, that continent represents the land of
the independence the settler obtains by the very fact
of setting his foot on its shore. The Jews of North
America have no history of their own; theirs is the
history of the freedom of that continent. American
Jews are none, but only Jews from all parts of Europe
who emigrated here, formed congregations and were
free and independent. In the seventeenth century,

Jews went to North and South America with the English and Portuguese: in the eighteenth century they joined in the struggle of the American colonies for their independence; and in the nineteenth America is the great commonwealth, where the Jewish portion of the population of Europe, being sick of Europe—some impelled by the spirit of adventure, others by rank despair—seek and find a harbor of refuge.''

In England, as we have seen, Menasseh Ben Israel of Amsterdam pleaded the cause of his co-religionists before Cromwell. Although this effort was then in vain, yet in 1666, under Charles II., permission to reside and practice their religion was granted to the Jews. Since that time Jews have become very numerous in England, which was and is to them a real home.

The Reformation opened a new and better era to the Jews. Not that the Reformers, personally, were much more tolerant to them than the Romish Hierarchy, but the very fact that the boasted Unity of the Church had received a serious blow, made people more inclined to toleration. Besides, since the invention of the printing-machine, the Jews had been engaged in publishing beautiful copies of the Hebrew Bible and of the Talmud. This brought their learning into prominence, and some of the leaders of public opinion were more friendly to them. Reuchlin, for instance, stood manfully up for the preservation of the Talmud. Luther, too, owed much to the Jews, for it was chiefly with the help of a Latin translation of Rashi's Commentary to the Old Testament made by Nicholas de Lyra, that he was enabled to translate the Old Testament from the original Hebrew.

The fury of persecution formerly directed against the Jews was now directed against heretics in the bosom of Christianity itself, and while the Jews were left alone, yet the anathema of public contempt, humiliation, and exclusion from every public or private connection, still all lay heavily upon them. Thus the period of 270 years, which intervened between the Reformation and the French Revolution, was of a monotonous character to the Jews, with the exception of a few instances, which attracted public attention. Thus in 1677 the pseudo-Messiah, Sabbathai Levi (born at Smyrna in 1625), died at Belgrade as a Mohammedan. Notwithstanding the apostacy of this pretender there were some who upheld his claims even after his death, and asserted that he was still the true Messiah, and that he was translated to heaven.

Some even of his most inveterate foes while living, espoused his cause after his death. A few years later this heresy appeared under a new form, and under the guidance of two Polish rabbis, who traveled extensively to propagate "Sabbathaism," which had its followers from Smyrna to Amsterdam, and even in Poland. In 1722 the whole sect was solemnly excommunicated in all the synagogues of Europe. In the year 1750, Jacob Frank, a native of Poland, made his appearance, who caused a schism in the synagogues of his native country, and founded the sect of the "Frankists."

The most extraordinary movement which occurred among the Jews in the eighteenth century was that of the sect termed the *Chasidin*, or hyper-orthodox Jews. Contemporary with the rise and progress of this sect there lived in Germany the famous Moses Mendelssohn, born in 1729 at Dessau, a man whose remarkable talents and writings constituted an era in the history of the modern Jews. The influence produced by the writings of Mendelssohn was to destroy all respect for the Talmud and the Rabbinical writers among the Jews who approved his opinions. Mendelssohn died in 1786.

Six years before Mendelssohn's death, Joseph II. had ascended the Austrian throne, and one of his first measures was an edict intended to ameliorate the condition of the Jews. In Austria Proper from the first establishment of the duchy in 1267, they were regarded as belonging to the sovereign of the country. In 1420 and 1460 persecutions broke out against them in Vienna. In 1553, Ferdinand I. had granted them the right to reside in the Austrian capital, but at a later date he expelled them. Maximilian II. recalled them, and Ferdinand II. permitted them, about the year 1620, to erect a synagogue in Vienna. In 1688 an edict appeared signifying the wish that they leave Vienna and the Duchy of Austria entirely; but in 1697 we find that the Jews had gradually returned in large numbers. After the accession of the Empress Maria Theresa their condition improved, and under Joseph II. they enjoyed equal rights and privileges with other subjects. They enjoyed these advantages until after the death of Joseph II. The reactionary spirit then prevailed in Austria, and many privileges were withdrawn.

As in Catholic Austria, so in Protestant Prussia, an amendment in the condition of the Jews began to appear and to develop itself as early as the eighteenth century. Under the Elector of Brandenburgh, Frederick William (1640-1688), the Jews had again an asylum and a safe abode in Prussia. During the reign of King Frederick I. the synagogue at Berlin was built. Frederick William, the father of Frederick the Great, was equally favorable to the Jews, although Frederick the Great is thought not to have looked favorably upon them. He did not persecute them, but, on the whole, they were treated as inferior to the other inhabitants of the country, and the whole community was considered responsible for the crimes of its individual members. The successor of Frederick the Great endeavored by new laws to effect a salutary change for the Jews ; the result was, that some of them attained to considerable wealth, but the majority of them retained a degraded and dependent position, which continued till toward the close of the eighteenth century. Mendelssohn, it is true, tried to elevate his people, and to bring about this task he was assisted by such men as Hartwig, Wessely, Isaac Enchel, David Friedländer and others. But the effect produced by his writings was precisely the same as that occasioned by the writings

of Maimondes six centuries earlier—to render
the Jews dissatisfied with their religion, and to
drive them either to the adoption of total in-
fidelity on the one hand, or of Christianity on
the other. The latter was the case with his
children.

The French Revolution marked a new era
in the history of the Jews. Not only the
Jews, but also the Christian, or, more properly
speaking, the civilized world, had become
intoxicated with the idea of reforming every-
thing. Several writers, as Dohm and Grégoire,
advocated the regeneration of the Jews, and the
French revolution furnished an opportunity
of realizing some of their ideas. The Jews
had been much neglected or cruelly oppressed,
but now a new system of legislation commenced. On September 27, 1791, the
French National Assembly declared them
citizens of France. On September 2, 1796,
a similar decree was passed in Holland.

Napoleon, when in the zenith of his power,
perceiving the spirit that was stirring in the
Jewish mind, conceived the idea of turning it
to his own advantage. He thought that the
Jews, existing in considerable numbers in
most parts of the world, understanding all
languages, possessing great wealth and en-

dowed with talents, might prove useful allies
in his plan of universal empire. He undertook the vast project of giving these scattered
fragments a center of unity in their long lost,
but never forgotten, national council—the
Sanhedrin. His idea was that all Jews in
the world would obey the Sanhedrin, and
that this body, with its seat at Paris and appointed by himself, would be governed by
him. He clearly saw that with the old fash-
ioned Jews he could effect nothing. The
land of their love was Palestine, their hope
the Messiah, and God their legislator. He
knew that to them their religion was every-
thing, and his decorations of the Legion of
Honor worse than nothing, yea, an abomina-
tion. To make use of the Jews it was necessary to reform them, and he perceived in
the nation a large party, ready and willing,
though upon different principles, to be the
agents in effecting this reform. And though
Napoleon's intention was to make the decis-
ions of the Sanhedrin the religious law of all
the Jews in the world, yet he felt the inde-
cency of legislating for a religious body to
which he did not belong. He therefore
thought it necessary, at least to preserve an
appearance of permitting this body to reform

itself. On July 28, 1806, the French Sanhedrin began to sit, and nominated as president, Abraham Furtado, a Portuguese of Bordeaux. After the meetings were fully constituted, and were prepared for the transaction of business, Napoleon appointed commissioners to wait upon them, and to present to them twelve questions, to answer which was to be the first and principal occupation of the Sanhedrin. The answers given by this body were satisfactory to Napoleon, who convened another great Sanhedrin in 1807. To this assembly the Rabbis from various other countries, especially from Holland, were invited, in order that the principles promulgated by the body might acquire general authority among the Jews. The Jews throughout France were at first highly pleased at the interest taken by the emperor in their affairs. But their joy was soon afterward diminished by an edict which he issued in those provinces which bordered on the Rhine, and which restricted the Jews in their commercial affairs. Nevertheless, in Westphalia, Napoleon exerted a favorable influence by supporting the reformatory endeavors of Israel Jacobsohn, who devoted himself to the diffusion of education among his brethren by establishing

schools and a seminary for the proper instruc-
tion of teachers among them. The same
Jacobsohn also undertook a reform in the
public worship. The temple which he built
at his own expense at Seesen, he furnished
with an organ, a choir of the school children,
and commenced regular preaching in German.
This was the first instance since the destruction of the Temple that instrumental music
was introduced into Jewish worship. The
Rabbinic Jews regarded the playing upon
instruments as a labor, and therefore a dese-
cration of the Sabbath. But the reformed
Jews cared little for Rabbinic principles, and
hailed this change with enthusiasm. Subsequently temples were built at Berlin, Hamburg, Leipsic, and everywhere.

Beyond the borders of France, the principles set forth by the Sanhedrin found but a
faint echo, and soon met with positive opposition, especially in Germany and Holland.
It is true, that the French armies at their
invasion of the Netherlands in 1795, effected
the producing by degrees a complete emancipation of the Jews. Yet, strange as it
may appear, the emancipation was received
and estimated very differently by the Jews of
Holland than by those of France. With a

few exceptions, the Jews of Spain and Portugal, who were lovers of monarchy and aristocracy upon principle, and devotedly attached to the House of Orange, cared not for a so-called emancipation, which accorded very little with their political attachments and their religious opinions. Even the Jews of the German and Polish synagogues of Holland were little disposed to exchange their ancient Israelitish nationality, for the new political character offered to them by the Revolution. Only a small number, following the spirit of the age, formed a kind of political association under the title of *Felix Libertate*, which gave rise to a schism in the synagogue, which lasted till the reign of William I. From this association, the *Felix Libertate*, which had founded an independent synagogue, three deputies were sent to the Sanhedrin at Paris.

In the new Batavian Republic, founded in 1795, the opinions concerning the political equality of the Jews were divided. There were many admirers of the Revolution of 1789 in France, and that of 1795 in Holland, yet they were restrained by scruples of conscience from wishing for a complete naturalization of the Jews. Finally, however, the contrary opinion prevailed, and the change was made. Under the government, first of Louis Napoleon, and then of the House of Orange, the Jews of Holland became reconciled by degrees to their new political rights. After the restoration of the House of Orange to the government of Holland, the principle of absolute equality among all the inhabitants also remained unaltered.

In Belgium also, the Jews enjoyed equality in the sight of the law. In spite of the new political position of the Jews in Europe, constituting as it does a new epoch in history, the ancient barriers between the Jews and Christians could not be broken down. In Germany, for instance, the entire emancipation of the Jews, which in France had been established, as it were, in a moment, had to struggle for more than thirty years longer. Already before the Revolution of 1789, in the principal states of Germany measures were taken to secure to the Jews some rights, and to amend their condition. The French Revolution, and the influence of the French Imperial Government, considerably aided the cause of the Jews throughout a great part of Germany, especially in Westphalia, with its capital, Frankfort-on-the-Maine, and in Prus-

sia. The reign of King Frederick William
III. assured to the Jews, by the edict published March 11, 1812, the right and title of
Prussian citizens, with some restrictions and
conditions.

When the Congress of Vienna, in 1815, settled the affairs of Europe, the sixteenth article
imposed upon the Diet an obligation to take
the necessary measures for advancing the
social improvement of the Jews, and to obtain
for, and to secure to them the enjoyment of
all civil rights, on condition of their fulfilling
the duties connected with them. This pro-
posal met with intense opposition from many
quarters. The prejudices against the Jews
seemed to be intense, varying in their nature
and degree according to the different circum-
stances of the thirty-eight states into which
the Germanic body was divided. In the end
the Congress decided to leave the decision of
the matter to the legislation of the respective
states representing the confederation. When
this subject came up subsequently for discus-
sion in the legislative bodies of the several
states it was found that three distinct parties
existed, who might be termed the Conservative, the Historical, and the Revolutionary.
The Conservative party wished to leave things

in statu quo; the Historical appealed to history, and insisted upon making progress and
improvements in harmony with the necessities
of the age. The Revolutionary party, caring
for neither history nor religion, insisted upon
an entire revolutions of things, in which,
amid the cry of universal equality, liberty,
and fraternity, the Jew, should secure his
equal rights. The most famous of the Revolutionary party was Bruno Bauer, who openly
declared he wished not for the emancipation of
the Jews, but for their entire destruction and
extinction. The King of Prussia, in the
spirit of the historical party, published an
edict, according to which equality of rights
and duties was secured to the Jews, with some
exceptions. The year 1848, with its revolutionary principles, effected the full emancipation of the Jews in Germany, and ever since
they are found in parliament as well as in
universities, in schools as well as in courts,
etc. Of late a reaction has taken place
against the Jews of Prussia, the end of which
cannot yet be foreseen.

In England, Parliament passed in 1753 a
bill for the naturalization of the Jews; but in
the following year the bill was rescinded. But
in 1847 their equality before the law was de-

clared. In the Scandinavian countries the
Jews enjoy many liberties, but not their absolute emancipation. In Russia the Jewish
population have experienced, at different
times, various kinds of treatment, and up to
this day they undergo many vexations.—As
in Russia, the Jews experienced a diversified
fate in the territories of the Pontiff, varying
according to the peculiar disposition and
prejudices of the successive Popes. Under
Pius VII. (1816–1825) they enjoyed ample
protection and equal franchises; different,
however, it was under Leo XII., who reën-
forced old and obsolete bulls. Under Pius
IX., the *Ghetto* of the Jews at Rome was solemnly and publicly opened, and thus the wall
of distinction and separation between Jews
and Christians was removed. The Pope's example was followed by Charles Albert in
1848, who proclaimed perfect equality of
political rights to the Jews.

In Mohammedan countries—Asiatic and Af-
rican—the relation between the Jews on the one
hand, and the government and people on the
other, has progressed in exact proportion that
the influence of Christianity and the growth of
civilization have exercised on those countries.
Still great, however, is the contempt in which

Jews and Christians, and more particularly
the former, are held by Mohammedan popu-
lations. But on the part of the government
of the Viceroy of Eygpt and of the Sultan of
Constantinople, a gradually increasing favor
has been exhibited to the Jews. At one time
only, in 1840, an accusation was leveled against
the Jews in Syria, for having assassinated
Father Thomas, who for thirty years had
practiced medicine at Damascus, and who, as
had been reported, was last seen in the Jewish
quarter. A persecution against the Jews took
place, scenes of barbarity occurred, till at last
the representations of the European govern-
ments made an end to the cruelties.

Wherever Jews are to be found at present,
they enjoy liberties and privileges. Looking
at their religious state in Europe and America,
we find the Jews divided into three parties:
the strict orthodox, conservative, and reformed, or liberal. In Europe the synagogue
has produced a number of learned men, who
have enriched oriental literature and other
sciences. In America, the land of liberty,
the Jews have been less productive.

In our rapid survey we have glanced at the
past and present of the Jews. There exist at
this day about seven million Jews, scattered

all over the globe. "The destinies of this wonderful people, as of all mankind," says Dean Milman, "are in the hands of the All-wise Ruler of the Universe. His decrees will be accomplished, his truth, his goodness, and his wisdom vindicated."

www.ingramcontent.com/pod-product-compliance
Lightning Source LLC
Chambersburg PA
CBHW021431090426
42739CB00009B/1452